I BRC
MY HEART
LOVING YOU

N. Niami

I BROKE MY HEART LOVING YOU

Published by: Noor Niami

For information contact:
Noor Niami
www.noorniami.com

First Printing, 2021
ISBN: 978-0-6489327-5-8 (paperback)

"Sometimes it takes a heartbreak to shake us awake and help us see we are worth so much more than we're settling for."

Mandy Hale

Dedicated to you

Be brave enough to let go of what is hurting your heart and soul.

This is my intention for you and for the world.

"The shattering of a heart when being broken is the loudest quiet ever."

Carroll Bryant

I have never loved anyone as much as I have loved you. My love for you was beyond anything I have felt before. Loving you was all I could do because my heart couldn't do anything other than to love you. But in the end you broke the heart that loved you.

- Noor Niami

You were everything to me; my lover and my best friend all in one. You were all I ever wanted and all I ever needed. You were the reason behind my smile and happiness but you also became the reason behind my tears and sorrows. You were my beginning but you also were my end.

- Noor Niami

Loving you and leaving you has been the hardest thing my soul had to go through. I crushed the last pieces of my heart when I let you go because holding on was damaging me far more. I lost myself holding onto you. I hurt myself trusting you and I broke my heart loving you.

- Noor Niami

I gave you all of me but it was never enough. I gave you the best of me but it was never enough. I gave you everything in me but even then that wasn't enough. I walked away feeling not enough.

- Noor Niami

It was hurting me to let go and move on. It took time for me to accept that we will no longer be. My heart needed time to accept that it was over and although it was hurting me to let go, the pain of holding on was hurting me more.

- Noor Niami

You promised you wouldn't hurt me. You promised you would protect me and I really thought I was safe with you. But you tore me down and hurt me like no one else has ever done before. The person I loved the most was the person who hurt me the most and that person was you.

- Noor Niami

I knew there was going to be a time when I had to let you go. I knew it was going to happen but a part of me hoped it wouldn't. But I knew the day would come when I have to do the one thing I feared the most; break my heart by leaving you.

- Noor Niami

I put you on a pedestal; I raised and upheld you so high. So high that in the end even I couldn't reach you. You made me believe you were too good for me but the truth was I was too good for you.

- Noor Niami

You got used to mistreating me because you knew I was always going to be there; ready to forgive and give you another chance. And you were right because I gave you many chances to disappoint me with. And that's on me.

- Noor Niami

You took my love for granted and abused the heart that loved you. You tore me down when all I ever did was build you up. You crushed my heart into pieces and tore my soul apart. I couldn't understand how you claimed to love me when all you ever did was hurt me.

- Noor Niami

A part of me wished maybe one day it would happen. Maybe one day I will finally see you fight for me and do what it takes to be with me. Maybe one day you will love me the way I had loved you and maybe one day you would choose me as I have chosen you. Then I realised I was waiting for a day that was never going to be.

- Noor Niami

I couldn't control your loyalty no matter how loyal I was to you. In the end you did everything you promised you wouldn't do. You lied, you cheated, and you betrayed me and broke my trust. You betrayed someone who trusted you more than you deserved.

- Noor Niami

You know what I don't deserve? I don't deserve to question whether or not I am worthy of your love. You know what I do deserve? I deserve to be with someone who is ready to be with me wholeheartedly and not make me question my worth of being loved.

- Noor Niami

I wish you knew what you put me through. I wish you felt the pain you made me feel. I wish your heart broke the way you broke mine. Only then you'd understand how deep my pain was but until then you have no idea what you have put me through.

- Noor Niami

Walking away hurt me more than you'll ever know. Walking away from you tore my heart and soul apart. But you know what hurt me more? Seeing how easily you gave up on me when I would've never given up on you.

- Noor Niami

The reason why you hurt me more than I deserved was because I gave you more than you deserved. I loved you more than you deserved, I trusted you more than you deserved and I sacrificed for you more than you deserved. So you hurt me more than I deserved because I loved you more than you deserved.

- Noor Niami

I really thought what we had was real; everything we've been through, all the memories we made and the time we spent. I really thought all of it was real. But to my dismay nothing about you was ever real and though what we had may not have been real to you, it was very real to me.

- Noor Niami

My love for you blinded me; my love for you made me ignore how poorly you treated me. My love for you oppressed me and tormented me. My love for you was what hurt me because I loved someone who didn't love me.

- Noor Niami

You thought I was always going to be there so you took my love for granted and abused the heart that loved you. But you thought wrong because I finally built up the courage to break the last pieces of my heart and walk away from you.

- Noor Niami

How did you change from being the source of my happiness to the source of my pain? How did you become the reason I smiled but also the reason I cried? You were the source to my joy but also the source to my sorrow and the person I couldn't live without became the person I couldn't live with anymore.

- Noor Niami

If you understand anything then let it be this; I didn't just give up on you. I'm not the sort of person who just gives up on someone I love and especially not you. You were the closest thing to my heart and I wasn't just going to give up on that. So when I gave up on you; on us, you need to understand that it took everything that was left inside of me to leave you. So no, it wasn't easy; it was the hardest thing I had to do because it broke my heart leaving you while still loving you.

- Noor Niami

All this time I thought you were mine but truth be told; you were never mine to begin with. You were everyone else's but certainly not mine. And all this time I thought I'd lost you but it turns out I never had you and you cannot lose what you never had.

- Noor Niami

The more I tried loving you, the more you tried hurting me. As though you enjoyed seeing me hurt because seeing me weak made you feel powerful and strong. Then I knew you never truly loved me because if you loved me you wouldn't have hurt me and if you hurt me then you never really loved me.

- Noor Niami

Giving up on everything I wanted was heartbreaking for me. All my dreams, wishes and desires came crushing down in front of me. But my heart was already breaking and my soul crushing every day of me waiting for something I knew was never going to happen.

- Noor Niami

I knew my good heart was at the palm of your hands. And I knew you had the power to break it but a part of me really hoped you wouldn't.

- Noor Niami

I miss you yes, but I don't miss the person you are. I miss the person I fell in love with; the person I thought you were. I miss what we had but I don't miss how you made me feel.

- Noor Niami

I wish you knew the depth of my love for you. I wish you knew how deep that love ran through. I wish you knew that no one could ever love you like I loved you. I wish you knew because things would've been so different if you knew.

- Noor Niami

I didn't deserve all the pain you inflicted on me. I didn't deserve to be betrayed the way you betrayed me. And I really hope you will never hurt anyone else the way you've hurt me because no one deserves to go through what you've put me through.

- Noor Niami

You never really valued me because if you did you wouldn't have put yourself in a position to lose me. But thank you for not valuing me to teach me how to value myself and walk away from those who didn't.

- Noor Niami

I would have done anything for you. Nothing could've stopped me. I could have been with anyone else but I always chose you because I believed in you and didn't give up on you. No one could have stopped me but not if that someone was you. You gave up on me first and you left me with no choice but to give up on you too.

- Noor Niami

I had to break my own heart by leaving you because I couldn't handle having you break my heart every day I was with you. And no, I didn't walk away because I stopped loving you; I walked away because it was time for me to love myself.

- Noor Niami

Some days I feel like I am over it and have passed through the storm but some days it hits me all over again. Just when I think I have it under control, I fall apart again. Just when I think I'm doing okay, sorrow hits my soul again. I guess this is what healing is all about; nothing about it makes sense but I have to trust that I will be okay in the end.

- Noor Niami

I loved you more than anything in this world. I put you above all else. I raised you up to the highest highs but in the process you brought me down to the lowest lows. I spent all my time and effort in building you up but in the end I broke myself trying to fix you.

- Noor Niami

Just because you see me holding it together doesn't mean I'm not falling apart on the inside. If you look closely behind my smile, you will see a hurting and wounded heart. Take a closer look into my eyes and you might get a glimpse of my pain. The pain within me is tearing me apart and everything inside of me is falling apart.

- Noor Niami

How long did you expect me to wait for you? Did you expect me to wait all my life for a decision you were never going to make? I waited long enough; too long, and I gave you years of my life that I'll never get back. But enough was enough and your indecision helped me make a decision to walk away because no reason to stay is a good reason to leave.

- Noor Niami

In case you forgot how good I was to you; let me remind you. I was the one who loved you more than anyone in this world. I was the one who believed in you when you couldn't believe in yourself. I was the one who chose to see the best in you even at your worst. I was the one who chose to stay when everyone told me to leave. I was the one who stood by your side through your good days and bad days. I took on your darkness and made it my own. I was so good to you and I wish I could say the same thing about you.

- Noor Niami

Loving you and being apart from you was a living hell for me to go through. It felt as though I was dead even when I was alive.

- Noor Niami

Eventually I had to stop asking why you were hurting me and ask myself why I am letting you hurt me. I allowed you to hurt me time and time again because with each time I thought things might be different. But you let me down with every chance I gave you.

- Noor Niami

All this time I thought I was in need of you but I was actually in need of myself; in need of my own love for myself. My journey wasn't about finding you but it was about losing you to find me because somewhere along the line I lost myself holding onto you. So I needed to lose you to find me.

- Noor Niami

I knew something was off but I made the mistake of disregarding my own feelings maybe because a part of me wasn't ready to face the truth. Believing in lie seemed easier at the time but in the end it was a lie that cost me everything.

- Noor Niami

Loving you destroyed my heart because I emptied myself out of my own love to fill you. Loving you depleted me of anything good I ever had inside. I walked away feeling empty, unworthy and unloved.

- Noor Niami

The saddest thing about betrayal is that it comes from the people we love the most. You betrayed me because you made me believe it was going to be different this time. But again you made promises you knew you wouldn't keep.

- Noor Niami

Someday, someone will ask you about me and when they do I hope you find it in yourself to be honest and say the truth. 'She was the one who loved me more than anyone has ever done before and in return I broke her and hurt her more than anyone has ever done before.'

- Noor Niami

Don't blame circumstances for why we're apart and don't give me excuses for why you didn't fight to keep me. In the end it was your own fear that stopped you and you decided to give up because giving up was easier than fighting for what you wanted. You chose the easy way out and allowed your fear to get the best of us. And here we are living out the consequences of a decision you made.

- Noor Niami

I made the mistake of equating my self-worth and value with your inability to love and appreciate me. I made the mistake of seeing myself through your eyes and believing in your version of who I am. I sold myself short because I wanted you to value me without knowing my worth.

- Noor Niami

The hardest thing you will ever go through is watching your whole world fall apart and you can't do anything to stop it from falling. You spent so much time and energy building it up only for it to come crumbling down in a matter of minutes. Everything you had envisioned; the life you planned with them ceases to exist and somehow you have to get back up and start all over again. This will break your heart in many ways and crush your soul in a thousand more ways.

- Noor Niami

I used to think all these years I spent with you were a waste of time but now I know that nothing is ever wasted. If it didn't give me what I wanted; it certainly gave me what I needed. Valuable lessons I wouldn't have learned otherwise. Thank you for showing me that I am worth so much more than what I was settling for.

- Noor Niami

I didn't stop loving you; I just learned to love me more. And I don't regret loving you because in loving you and losing you I learned how to love myself and find me again.

- Noor Niami

You may have torn my world apart and broke me down but you also gave me the opportunity to rebuild something new; something far more beautiful than the life I had with you.

- Noor Niami

Thank you for not giving me what I needed from you and thank you for not being there when I needed you. You taught me that I am in need of myself and I will never put myself in a position to need anyone the way I needed you. And if you weren't there when I needed you the most, what makes you think I'll ever need you again?

- Noor Niami

You didn't love me; you just loved the idea of having me around whenever you needed me. You knew that I was always going to be there at your beck and call and your wishes were my commands. You loved being the center of my world yet I was nowhere to be found in yours. You didn't love me; you just loved the idea of me loving you.

- Noor Niami

Don't believe in mere words because words without actions are empty words. They can tell you they love you yet show you that they don't. Always believe in the way a person is treating you because how they treat you says a lot about their love for you.

- Noor Niami

I may have given you many chances; way more than you deserved and I may have let you stay in my life longer than you needed to and that's okay. At least now I can walk away knowing that I gave it my best. There is nothing else I could have done or said because I gave it my all and that's all I had to give.

- Noor Niami

Sometimes the people you came with cannot go with you to where you are headed. Some people will only be compatible with who you used to be not the person you are becoming. You need to accept that some people will only be a part of your past but cannot be a part of your future because their role in your life has finished.

- Noor Niami

I didn’t give up; I just had enough and there’s a difference between giving up and having enough. Having enough means I fought so hard, I tried so many times and yet it still wasn’t happening no matter how hard I tried. I had enough of being the only one trying and I had enough of being the only one fighting.

- Noor Niami

I owe myself the biggest apology for letting people hurt me and take my good heart for granted. I owe myself an apology for disregarding my own feelings to make others feel comfortable. I owe myself an apology for letting people stay in my life longer than they deserved. I am sorry.

- Noor Niami

There comes a time in your life when you have to self-reflect and ask yourself these questions. How long are you going to wait for something that you know may never happen? How long are you going to put your life on hold for someone who may never be ready? How long are you willing to wait for the impossible to happen? You've already waited long enough and nothing has happened. It's time to let go.

- Noor Niami

Just because you couldn't see my worth didn't mean I am not worthy. I've always been worthy and it was never about you seeing my worth but about me learning that I am worthy of so much more.

- Noor Niami

Love is never a mistake but loving the wrong person is. It wasn't love that broke my heart; it was loving you that broke me. True love does not hurt; loving the wrong person does.

- Noor Niami

There were so many times when I was willing to give up on everything just to be with you. Everything that I cared about was nothing in comparison to you. I was willing to lose it all than lose you. But all this time I was scared of losing someone who didn't care about losing me.

- Noor Niami

Saying goodbye to you; to the one I loved, broke my heart beyond repair. I knew that my life would never be the same without you. I knew that I wasn't going to be the same person I once was. Loving you and leaving you has been the hardest thing for me to do but I had to let you go to save what was left of my soul.

- Noor Niami

It hurt because it was real. It was hard because it was real. It broke my heart because it was real. And though it may not have been real to you; it was very real to me.

- Noor Niami

I learned that I can't force things or control the uncontrollable so I stopped forcing pieces that don't fit in my life. I learned to let things go and let things be and trust that everything will work itself out for me and what's meant to be always will be.

- Noor Niami

I couldn't love you into loving me because love is a choice; a decision we make. I made mine in loving you but I couldn't make you choose to love me because it was a decision you needed to make. But you were incapable of loving someone other than yourself.

- Noor Niami

We both made mistakes. My mistake was thinking that you would change but you didn't. Your mistake was thinking that I would never change but I did. You didn't believe that one day I was going to find the strength to walk away from you but I did because I finally realised I deserved better.

- Noor Niami

There's a difference between loving someone and doing what it takes to be with them. You say you love me but you're doing nothing to be with me. I would rather be with someone who does what it takes to be with me than someone who tells me they love me.

- Noor Niami

Some people move on quicker than others but moving on for me was never easy. Letting go was always a struggle because I held on dearly to those I loved. I knew this was going to take time because breaking free from my broken self was going to be a journey rather than a destination.

- Noor Niami

The hardest thing I've had to do was to let go of what was hurting my heart and soul. I had to let go of everything that was weighing me down and learn how to fly and rise above the ashes that were meant to bury me. I became the fire that once tried to consume me and climbed the mountain that tried to crush me.

- Noor Niami

I never knew how strong I really was until I had to forgive you for breaking my heart without any apology or remorse. It takes a strong heart to love but a stronger heart to continue to love after it's been broken and forgive someone who wasn't sorry.

- Noor Niami

What would you know about heartbreak and pain? You see, heartbreak changes you and pain molds you into someone new. So unless you have grown and evolved you cannot change. The same person who broke my heart is the same person who is breaking someone else's heart today. So no, you don't know anything about heartbreak or pain. You will do what you have always done but this time it won't be done to me.

- Noor Niami

I don't like saying this very often but sometimes the truth must be told lest you diminish my pain or what I've been through. You broke me; not once, but time and time again. You betrayed me; no once, but time and time again. You let me down and disappointed me and here's the best part of it all; I no longer care if this makes you feel uncomfortable because I am done denying my own feelings for you.

- Noor Niami

Despite everything you've put me through I haven't been able to love anyone else other than you. I wish I understood why or how my heart could still love you. But then I realised the heart that loved you will never hate you and I can't force my heart to do something it wasn't taught to do.

- Noor Niami

Crying was the only way I could express my pain because no words were able to describe how broken I was. I crumbled and shattered into scattered pieces and I no longer wanted to fake that I was okay because I wasn't. I couldn't do it anymore; pretending that I was unbreakable when everything in me was breaking.

- Noor Niami

I was heartbroken and sad when you gave up on me. You gave up on me and us so easily. You gave up on the one person who would have never given up on you.

- Noor Niami

We may have settled for less than what we deserved because we didn't know our true self-worth and value and that's okay, rarely anyone does when they begin. And it takes a bad relationship to teach you what a good relationship is and to show you that you are worthy of so much more than the relationship you tried settling for.

- Noor Niami

It's not that you are unworthy of love; it's just that you've given your good heart to bad people. You loved the wrong people; people who didn't appreciate the beauty of your good heart. You are worthy of love but you must start with your own love for yourself because self-love is the best love you can give yourself.

- Noor Niami

Although it was you who hurt me; it was I who allowed it. I am to blame in all this too because I let you get away with a lot. I allowed you to hurt me by sticking around and giving you another chance yet once again. I guess a part of me wanted to believe you were capable of changing and becoming a better man.

- Noor Niami

We had many problems but do you know what our main problem was? I cared too much and you didn't care enough. I gave too much and you didn't give enough. I loved too much and you didn't love enough. I did so much and you didn't do enough.

- Noor Niami

A part of me really believed that I couldn't live without you. The thought of being without you tormented me because I couldn't see myself with anyone else other than you. I thought I wasn't going to survive without you in my life but look at me now. I am living and doing more than surviving; I am thriving and living my best life without you.

- Noor Niami

I cared about you; a lot, but I care about me too and I need to save myself from you. Who would have thought the person I loved the most was going to be the same person I needed to run away from to save my soul?

- Noor Niami

Loving you and needing you are two different things. At one stage I loved you and I needed you. And today; I can love you but not need you because the only person I am in need of is myself.

- Noor Niami

You didn't lie to protect me; you lied to protect yourself. You didn't lie to save me; you lied to stop me from finding out the truth. No matter how loyal I was to you it wasn't going to change your unfaithfulness towards me. You did everything you wanted to do and I couldn't stop you but I certainly stopped myself from being with a liability like you.

- Noor Niami

I let you get the best of me, I let you control me and in fact I let you break me. But I can finally say that I am letting go and moving on because what is the point of holding onto someone who is not holding onto you? We both lost; I lost someone who didn't care about me and you lost someone who actually cared about you.

- Noor Niami

Don't look at my attitude and ask me why I have changed towards you. Don't question why I am a different person than the person you once knew. But look at what you have done to push me to change towards you because believe it or not you are looking at the effect of something you caused.

- Noor Niami

I didn't walk away because I stopped loving you; I walked away still loving you. But I couldn't do it anymore. I couldn't keep up with the constant fighting, the arguing, the crying, the begging, the shouting. The sleepless nights I spent drowning myself in my tears. I just couldn't do it anymore. I couldn't keep up with the mind games you played on me; the emotional and mental turmoil you put me through. So no, I didn't walk away because I didn't love you; I walked away because I couldn't do it anymore.

- Noor Niami

And someday you will realise that I was everything you wanted and hoped for. That I was the one you have been searching and looking for. And you will look back and regret everything you've put me through but by then it'll all be too late.

- Noor Niami

You changed me. You changed who I was and I will never be that person again. I used to be sad knowing I wasn't going to be the old me again but then I was glad. I was glad not being the old me again because the person I have become today will never be with a person like you again.

- Noor Niami

You know what confused me the most? Was you telling me you loved me but wouldn't fight to be with me. You said you loved me but you were hurting me and I couldn't understand how could someone who claims to love me hurt me? You didn't love me; you just loved yourself and the idea of having someone loving you and that's when all else made sense.

- Noor Niami

I didn't learn what love is being with you but I certainly learned what love is *not*. Love doesn't hurt you; love should bring the best in you. Love doesn't break you and tear you down; love should build you up. Love shouldn't be exhausting; love should be effortless and free. Love doesn't empty you, drain you and oppress you; love should fill you, uplift you, encourage you and liberate you. I know what love is not all thanks to you.

- Noor Niami

Everybody has a breaking point and you pushed me into mine. I was done with making excuses to justify your poor behaviour and actions. I was done with listening to your reasons which somehow were all my fault. I was done with pretending to be okay when everything in me was not. I had enough of wishing things were going to change and accepted that they were not. We all have a breaking point and you pushed me into mine.

- Noor Niami

Now I know why I needed to be broken. I needed to break so I could learn a new way of living and being. I needed to break to find out how strong I really was. I needed to break to know what I am truly made out of. I needed to reach rock bottom so that I can learn how to fly and rise to the top. I bless my journey and what I have been through because I was given the opportunity to rebuild something new.

- Noor Niami

I couldn't fathom the idea of you not being a part of my future. I didn't want to accept that you were just going to be a part of past and that's part of the reason why I held on for longer than I needed to. My heart wasn't ready to accept what my mind already knew and this was the greatest battle I had to go through.

- Noor Niami

You abandoned me in times when I needed you the most. All I wanted was for you to be there just as I have always been there for you. I wanted you to be around not just on the good days but most importantly on the bad days too. Yet you were nowhere to be found because you abandoned me when I needed you the most. You were never there for me just as I was always there for you and you taught me not to need anyone the way I needed you.

- Noor Niami

I fought so hard and for so long. I tried so many times and I gave it my all. I really wanted us to work out but it just wasn't happening. I drained myself, I was exhausted, and I was tired of being the only one fighting for us. Things might've been different if you actually fought for me too but you didn't fight to be with me and that's because you didn't care about losing me.

- Noor Niami

It baffled me how you go on hurting me and then pretend to be the one hurt. You would accuse me of the very things you were doing and make me feel guilty for something I didn't do. You made me question myself thinking I was going crazy and made me apologize even when I didn't do anything wrong. You made me believe in all your lies but thankfully the truth always prevails and I finally found out the truth about you.

- Noor Niami

Despite how you made feel and everything I have been through, I can finally say that I am proud of the woman I have become today. Because I went through hell becoming her and I paid dearly for who I am today. The new me has cost me my old self and unless you have been through a spiritual death and rebirth then you have no idea what it took for me to be who I am today.

- Noor Niami

Life has taught me that I don't always need a plan and I don't need to have all the answers. I don't need to understand everything I'm going through but I do need to trust it. I learned to just breathe, let go, trust and let things unfold how they need to. I don't need to know where I am going or when I will get there. I just need to worry less and trust more knowing that in the end everything is going to be okay; I am going to be okay.

- Noor Niami

You have to go through what you don't want so you know what you do want. You needed to be in that bad relationship to know what a good relationship is. You had to be with the wrong person so you can end up with the right person. The journey you're on now and everything you're going through is leading you to what your heart truly desires. It's all part of the plan, trust it.

- Noor Niami

And one day I will be with someone who will love me for who I am and not who they want me to be. I will be with someone who will see my worth and appreciate my value. I will be with someone who knows how special I am and sees the beauty in all my scars. But until that day; I will be that someone to myself because I need to find these things in me before I can find them in anyone else.

- Noor Niami

In the end your purpose in my life was to heal me from that which already existed within me since the beginning of time. You didn't break me; I was already broken. You didn't hurt me; I was already hurting. You echoed in resonance that which already existed within me and you were the mirror that reflected back to me the things I couldn't see. You brought my darkness to light and for that I thank you and I bless everything I've been through.

- Noor Niami

"Your greatest responsibility is to love yourself and to know you are enough."

Unknown

A Message From the Author

Don't let your love for someone else be greater than the love you have for yourself because the moment you love someone more than yourself you will lose yourself. Don't lose yourself for anyone else; you are far more worthy of the love you are trying to give everybody else. Our relationship with ourselves will set the tone and expectation to every other relationship in our lives. So be sure to treat yourself how you want others to treat you. Give yourself what you are trying to get others to give you and then you will realise the only person you were ever in need of is *yourself*.

You are worthy of being loved and cherished, don't let someone's inability to love you make you think otherwise. Be brave enough to let go of what is no longer serving you and patient enough to wait for what you deserve.

With love,
Noor

About the Author

Noor Niami is an author, spiritual mentor and an entrepreneur but above all she is a woman of God and a believer. Christ alone defines the woman she is and her identity is built purely on Him. Her passion to help others has become her purpose in life and she is determined to empower those who have been hurt and heal the broken-hearted by sharing her personal journey and experiences. Coming from a place of brokenness herself she knows what it feels like to be in that dark place desperately waiting to see the light at the end of the tunnel. It wasn't until she refused to wait any longer and decided to become the light she needed instead. And from there on her mission to empower people around the world began. She is determined be a living testimony to God's unfailing love, grace, and mercy. And she wants to assure you that the pain you've been feeling now can't compare to the joy that is coming. (Romans 8:18)

For more information visit:

www.noorniami.com

Lightning Source UK Ltd.
Milton Keynes UK
UKHW010818160821
388939UK00004B/534